RISE

A 30 day devotional for women of faith

TO YOUR

Who want to shine their light

PURPOSE

In the business world.

WRITTEN BY
BRANDIE THOMAS & NATALIE LAWSON

Energy4PR
Publishers
"your story;
their hope"

Book Cover: Skyler Lawson
Interior Design by Energy4PR Publishers.

Paperback ISBN: 978-1-63732-036-5
Digital ISBN: 978-1-63732-037-2

Rise To Your Purpose:
A 30-Day Devotional for Women of Faith
Who Want to Shine Their Light
in the Business World

Connect:
https://www.VictoriousEntrepreneursRising/**Rise**

Table of Contents

Part 1: Identity

Part 2: Core Values

Part 3: Rising Up

Table of Contents

Part 3: Rising Up (cont.)

Part 4: Closing Letter & Resources

Closing Letter from Brandie & Natalie

3 Bonus Resources

"In a world full of competing platforms and social noise, the temptation to hustle and 'prove ourselves' is real. Maybe it's a God-given vision, but we're holding it too tightly and feeling crushed! Brandie and Natalie's devotional, *Rise To Your Purpose*, isn't just timely, it's critical! The perspectives shared, and most importantly the heart through which they share them, will give every business owner & entrepreneur practical ways to thrive in their identity, find rest through surrendered control, and rise up to reclaim the joy in their purpose!"

**- Tim Hooper, Connection Coach &
Author of *Got Energy?***

"Nothing inspires me more than women who take a stand for other women. Natalie & Brandie are two of those women. Not only do they have incredible knowledge in business, building a brand and social marketing, they also share their knowledge of the Word of God seamlessly. Both of these incredible women are authentic and transparent, which makes them even more magnetic. This book will serve as a beacon of hope and a light directing others women on their path while pointing to the Savior. If there was ever a time to encourage other women to "Rise To Their Purpose", it is now. Well done ladies, many lives will be dramatically impacted by this book!"

**- Michelle Schaffer, CEO & Founder
of GPA (Girl Power Alliance)**

"I remember when I began my entrepreneurial journey, I was full of doubt, fear and uncertainty. It took me a long time to overcome those limiting beliefs and work through the destructive habits that were holding me back from achieving what I wanted in my life for myself and my family. I wish I would have had this daily devotional at that time in my journey. To have a resting place to turn to, a place where I could be reminded of who I was and to constantly be encouraged to go after my goals and dreams...and become the light God needs me to be in this world. This devotional is an essential tool for anyone needing an overhaul in their spiritual life as they navigate the ups and downs of entrepreneurship."

- Kimberly Olson, Self-Made Millionaire &
Best-Selling Author of *The Goal Digger*
& *Why Balance is B.S.*

"What you hold in your hands are 30 treasures of Heaven that Brandie and Natalie have discovered by walking through life and several businesses with the Lord - and by helping so many other strong women over the years to do the same. I invite you to allow their spirits to speak into yours, to allow your heart to be ministered to and loved on by your Father who has been seeking your face. Be encouraged to step into what you were created to bring into this world as Brandie and Natalie highlight the specific Scriptures through which God has always been calling you. Calling you to remember your identity. Calling you to choose an abundant life. Calling you to rise to your purpose!"

- Ashley Nicole, Spiritual Rest Coach
of the *Rest Intensive* program

Dedication

This devotional is for women who love Jesus and want to grow more intimately in their relationship with Him. Maybe along the way to your God sized dream, you have gotten out of alignment and/or are unclear on your purpose. We want you to know that life is not all trials and tribulations. As your belief in Him grows, and as you step into our Holy Spirit Empowerment, there is a life of abundance and victory waiting for you.

So, are you ready to rise?

This devotional is dedicated to our husbands, Jeremy Thomas and Skyler Lawson, who have always encouraged and held space for us to rise as entrepreneurs. Thank you for empowering us to step into our purpose and vision and for never holding us back. We love you!

We also dedicate this to our parents, Tammy and Lindy Unger, for always encouraging us in all of our endeavors. Thank you for your love and guidance throughout our life and helping to form the women we are today.

*Finally, we dedicate this devotional to our Purpose Partners. You are the inspiration behind this devotional and everything we do through our brand, **Victorious Entrepreneurs Rising**. We believe in you and know that together we can do great things for the Kingdom.*

Foreword

"For we are God's masterpiece, created in Christ Jesus to do good works, which God prepared in advance for us to do."
Ephesians 2:10

This is who Brandie Thomas and Natalie Lawson are, God's masterpieces, who are doing the good works God prepared and planned for them to do. They are here in this time and place especially for you. They have created this devotional to help you realize that's who you are too. You are God's masterpiece - created to do good works already planned especially for you. This beautiful devotional is designed to help you seek God and know exactly what those plans are...to encourage your heart and soul to pursue your unique God given calling as you create a world impact as a kingdompreneuer.

I have been given the privilege to know both Brandie and Natalie their entire lives, watching them grow through cat fights to becoming best friends to ultimately eternal sisters in Christ. As I was taught by their great, great "Aunt Jean", I was given the privilege to pray for them even before they were born, that they would "be raised up to be strong Christians who love, serve and obey God". I am privileged to be their mom. My heart cannot express the blessings of these privileges, to see these prayers answered over and over again as they continue to inspire me to also pursue my calling as a kingdomprenuer.

It is my prayer for each of you that you will be as blessed and inspired as I have been as you lean into who you truly are, into your unique callings and God given purposes. May you realize the deep love and full potential that God has abundantly prepared for you. May you become the kingdom impact you were always created to be and may you always be encouraged in hope.

~ **Tammy Unger**
Mom Blessed Beyond Measure
Encourager of Hope
Life Mentor

Our Letter to You

Dear Purpose Partner,

We are so grateful for you. Even if we haven't yet met, we know that the Lord has crossed our paths for a reason. We are honored to be able to partner with you in faith and business as you rise to your purpose.

We wrote this with you in mind. We know how challenging the business world can be. As women, we are so used to being in control of a lot of things and having to manage lots of different responsibilities.

When it comes to the business world though, we find that the results are often out of our control. It can be easy to let comparison and fear conquer us day in and day out or to let our self worth be caught up in a rank or promotion.

What we've grown to learn is that it's about learning to surrender it all to the Lord. This includes our finances, our worries, our timeline, and our results. We realize that we must truly partner with Him as our CEO and allow God to guide us. "We can make our plans, but the Lord's purpose will prevail."

As you continue on your journey, there will be things that come up in your life and business that can bring up new limiting beliefs and resistance. Listen to your spirit during these times to know what it is you need to do and hold fast to the vision that's been placed in your heart. Don't allow distractions or today's circumstances blind you to the possibilities of tomorrow.

Stay true to your core values, allow yourself time to rest, and remember not to put so much pressure on yourself.

Through it all, abide in Him and keep Jesus at the center. Anyone can give you tools and strategies, but ultimately you have to align with your spirit and be lead by the Word. When you seek Him, we promise He will reveal it to you.

"Every branch in Me that does not bear fruit, He takes away; and every branch that bears fruit, He prunes it so that it may bear more fruit. You are already clean because of the word which I have spoken to you. Abide in Me, and I in you. As the branch cannot bear fruit of itself unless it abides in the vine, so neither can you unless you abide in Me." John 15:2-6

As we begin these next 30 days together, we hope that you know how loved you are and the value that you have. It's time to come out of the shadows so you can shine your light in the business world.

Prepare your heart and mind to receive the blessings for more of what God has for you. Ask Him to reveal what He wants you to discover about yourself and His word over these next 30 days.

Don't hold this transformation and knowledge inside. Share the message, spread the gospel, and come boldly and confidently into your space of influence knowing that you have the ability to be a fearless faith influencer and world changer.

So now it's time, Purpose Partner. Let's dive in. As you read through, we want you to take time to read the scriptures in your own Bible. Then complete the reflection questions to get the most out of your time.

We'd love to hear from you. Share about your journey on social media by using **#risetoyourpurpose** so we can all rise together.

This is just the beginning of Rising to Your Purpose, and

we thank you for allowing us to be a part of your journey.

See you on Day 1! Let's Rise!

Praying for you,

Brandie and Natalie

P.S. Be sure to grab your bonuses at the link below. Along with these bonuses, you'll receive our 4-part mini-course: *Building Your Kingdom-Impact Network-Marketing Business.* You'll also receive an invitattion to join us in our *Rise to Your Purpose Signature Program.* We hope to continue partnering with you in faith and business.

FREE resources:

1. Creating Your Scripture-Based, Daily Affirmations

2. Building Your Kingdom Impact Network Marketing Business

3. Rise to Your Purpose Spotify Playlist

Visit https://www.VictoriousEntrepreneursRising/Bonus

Join us in our Purpose Partner **Community**:

https://www.facebook.com/groups/victoriousentrepreneuers

Join us in Rise to Your Purpose:

https://www.VictoriousEntrepreneursRising/Rise

Time to Rise

Day 1

"Arise, for it is your task, and we are with you;
be strong and do it."
Ezra 10:4

I (Brandie) have been where you are now, hearing that still small voice inside of my heart telling me it's time. It's time to move. It's time to stand up and stand out. You are not designed to look or act like the world. I was terrified of what other people would think, what they would say, and doubted the still small voice inside of me. Are you sure this is for me? Are you sure you have the right girl?

Here I am, finally! I didn't know all the things, have all the answers, or always feel qualified for this calling while on my journey. I had doubts, limiting beliefs, and fears. I questioned God's calling. Still, every time I received confirmation through God's provisions, His resources, and His Holy Spirit's guiding information.

Just like God called Nehemiah to build the wall of Jerusalem, He's calling you to build up His kingdom. You can do this through your business, your job, your family, and in any circle of influence. Don't limit yourself. He will give you the resources you need for your journey. Release the results to the Lord, and let him guide and direct your steps.

"You have been called by your King to rise up!"

It's time. It's time for you to stop shrinking. It's time for you to stop asking for permission to step into your calling. It's time for you to stop living up to everyone else's expectations of who they think you should be and what they think you should do. Release anything that is not really you so you can begin stepping into who He's created you to be.

You have been called by your King to rise up! This is your divine task. You are equipped with Holy Spirit empowerment, strength, and courage. You have a purpose. You have dreams and passions that have been placed in your heart by your Creator. Listen to that calling on your heart to rise. Will it be easy? No, but we can have peace on our journeys because Jesus says, "I have told you these things, so that in me you may have peace. In this world you will have trouble. But take heart! I have overcome the world."

Release and Receive

Read

Ezra 10:4 | Nehemiah 2 | John 16:33

Reflect

What would you be doing if you knew you
could not fail and had full support?

_____

_____

_____

_____

_____

_____

_____

_____

_____

Where are you feeling the Holy Spirit
move inside you?

_____

_____

PRAY

Praise | Repent | Ask | Yay

Father, thank you for giving me a servant's heart. Thank you for putting a spirit in me to rise up and become all that you are calling me to become. Forgive me for shrinking and not believing in myself the way that you believe in me. I ask that you give me your Holy Spirit empowerment to stand in my truth and take the next step you are guiding me to take. I praise you for the blessings that are coming my way.

I thank you for all that you are doing ahead of me that I do not even see yet.

You are a good, good Father.

In your name I pray, Amen.

Well Done, Good & Faithful Servant

Day 2

"His master replied, 'Well done, good and faithful servant! You have been faithful with a few things; I will put you in charge of many things. Come and share your master's happiness!'" - Matthew 25:23

How many times have you thought to yourself:
"I have nothing to offer the world."

"No one wants to hear what I have to say."

"I am not qualified to do what I feel called to do."

"I am not talented enough."

"What if I don't have what it takes?"

Did you ever let these thoughts stop you from going after that nudge or calling in your heart? Or did you go on in spite of those doubts and press on towards the goal and run the race?

God has given you talents, skills, and qualities that you can use for kingdom impact. Sometimes it's easier said than done, and you let your fear get in the way of serving others with the blessings you have through your business.

In the Parable of the Talents (Matthew 25:14 - 30), the Master gave each of his servants bags of gold **according to their ability**. The servant with the five bags of gold went out and doubled his blessings as did the servant who was given three bags of gold, but the

> *"God has given you special talents, gifts, and blessings according to your abilities."*

one who was given one bag hid it in the ground. When the Master returned, he called the servant who did not use what he was given wisely "wicked and lazy" instead of "good and faithful" like he called the other two who duplicated their earnings.

God has given you special talents, gifts, and blessings according to your abilities. You are meant to share them in the world and use them for His glory.

Not hide what you have been blessed with from those who you have been called to serve! Your abilities, stories, and journey will be shared differently from others who might even have a similar message as you. What makes it different is YOU. Specific people will resonate with you. It does not make one better or worse than the other. There is only one you.

You are meant for more. No one in this world can duplicate your specific purpose. No one can serve quite like you do. The enemy will tell you lies to make you feel like you are unworthy and you are not brave or don't have what it takes, but do not listen! The world needs YOU! The world needs what you have to offer!

Don't push away God's blessings! Receive them and do something good with Him, and you will get to hear "Well done, good and faithful servant!"

"No one in this world can duplicate your specific purpose!"

Read

Matthew 25:14 - 30

Reflect

What can your "kingdom impact" be with your business?

_____

_____

_____

_____

_____

_____

_____

_____

_____

_____

_____

_____

_____

PRAY

Praise | Repent | Ask | Yay

Father, thank you so much for the special abilities and talents you have specifically given to me. What an honor it is to know that you CHOSE me to be in this world at this point in time. You created me to serve your kingdom now. Forgive me for hiding my talents from the world and not living up to my full potential. You believe in me and created me to be the special person I am. Remove the self doubt and help me to decipher the lies that the enemy is telling me to stop from doing the purpose you have called me to live out. I know I am here to build relationship with You. Thank you for always being there for me and for providing me with everything I need in order to do the work you have created me to fulfill. I praise your name for all the blessings you will bring into my life and for the blessings you will use me to bring to my community.

In your name I pray, Amen.

You Have an Appointment to Keep

Day 3

"Before I formed you in the womb I knew you; before you were born I set you apart; I appointed you as a prophet to the nations."
Jeremiah 1:5

Do you know how special you are? Do you realize what an impact you can make each day you show up and stand in your purpose? If you have ever had someone tell you a negative comment or said you could not do something, then I(Brandie) know how difficult it can be to believe you do not matter. Maybe you have thought the world may be better without you at times. Maybe you think, what does it even matter if you don't fulfill your purposes anyway?

Sister! God chose YOU and knew YOU before YOU

were born. He chose YOU to stand apart. He chose YOU to go into the world and share His love.

You have a unique story, a unique desire that you are called to share with the world around you. Your story will not look like what the world's version expects it to look like. That's a GOOD thing. You are meant to be in the world, not of the world. So don't be fooled or distracted when the "world" looks at you with a

"Sister! God chose YOU!"

funny face or makes a cheeky comment. "Do not become weary in doing good," sister. We are to be about the Father's business, not tied up in everyone else's. Take His heart into the world, "for at the proper time, you will reap a harvest if you do not give up."

You have an appointment to keep. You have been ordained by God to go into the world through your business and share your story with your audience. You have been blessed with followers, you have been blessed with influence, you have been blessed with business savvy. You have Holy Spirit Empowerment working for you and God is your CEO. You've got this!

Read

Luke 2:48-49 | Galatians 6:9 | Jeremiah 1:5 -10

Reflect

What is something unique that sets you apart
in your industry or business?

_____

_____

_____

_____

_____

_____

_____

_____

_____

_____

How can you stand in your unique truth to be a
light for others and build kingdom impact?

_____

_____

_____

_____

_____

_____

_____

_____

_____

_____

PRAY

Praise | Repent | Ask | Yay

"Spirit, lead me where my trust is without
borders. Let me walk upon the waters wherever
you would call me. Take me deeper than my feet
could ever wander and my faith will be made
stronger in the presence of Savior." Amen

Prayer from Oceans by Hillsong United

Are You Ready to Become the Woman You Aspire to Be?

Day 4

"You, Lord, give perfect peace to those who keep their purpose firm and put their trust in you. Trust in the Lord forever; he will always protect us." - Isaiah 26:3-4

God chose YOU so that you might go and bear fruit (John 15:16).

That's why you've felt the calling to do more and be more. You have a message to share. In order to do that and be given discernment, learn to seek Him above all else for "God is doing a new thing in your life."

It is so important to stay in constant communion with Him so that he can direct you on this new journey.

Offer to Him your time, your heart, and your business so you can embrace the extraordinary life He has for you. Remember abundance is the very heart of who God is. He lavishes in you and your joy. Come to Him with joyful expectation knowing that through His Spirit in you, you are capable and qualified to lead, serve, and to sell your products or services.

"Stay in constant communion with Him so that He can direct you."

Let your requests and prayers be made known to him. When you "delight yourself in the Lord, He will give you the desires of your heart."

So as you begin discovering more of your purpose and how He has called you to serve, know that you can show up as a fearless influencer and world changer. You are a beloved daughter of God. When you recognize that God has placed you as His partner to bring His influence into your community and industry, that is when you see change.

Come to Him with open hands and heart ready to give and receive. Make a commitment to become authentic, transparent, and wholehearted servant leaders. Mark 3:13 says, "Jesus went up on a mountainside and called to him those he wanted, and they came to Him."

Now is your time to come and let your light shine.

"Come to Him with joyful expectation knowing that you are capable and qualified!"

Read

Isaiah 26:3-4 | John 15:16 | Isaiah 43:19

Psalm 37:4 | Mark 3:13

Reflect

What would it look like for me to go and
bear fruit?

_____

_____

_____

_____

_____

_____

_____

_____

_____

What business requests do I need to
make known to God?

_____

_____

_____

_____

_____

_____

_____

_____

_____

_____

PRAY

Praise | Repent | Ask | Yay

Father, we praise you for our gifts and for those
you have planned for us to lead and serve. We
pray for peace, confidence, and discernment
as we discover our unique brand and mission.
We ask that we not be sidetracked by the shiny
objects that can tempt us or the lies of the enemy
that can tell us we aren't good enough or qualified. Thank you Lord for calling me and for
preparing this future with hope.

In your name, Amen.

Rooted in Your Identity

Day 5

"Forget the former things; do not dwell on the past. See, I am doing a new thing! Now it springs up; do you not perceive it? I am making a way in the wilderness and streams in the wasteland."
Isaiah 43:18-19

For you are a people holy to the Lord your God. The Lord your God has chosen you out of all the peoples on the face of the earth to be his people, His treasured possession. The Lord did not set his affection on you and choose you because you were more numerous than other peoples, for you were the fewest of all peoples. But it was because the Lord loved you and kept the oath he swore to your ancestors that he brought you out with a mighty hand and redeemed you from the land of slavery, from the power of Pharaoh king of Egypt." Deuteronomy 7:6-8

Reread that again if you need to. What does that make you feel or think?

As we mature and grow as daughters of Christ, one thing we can become secure in is knowing how deeply treasured and loved we truly are.

You see ... God is love.

"Because God is love, you are loved!"

He sets his affection on you. Because God is worthy, you have worth. Because God is love, you are loved. As you grow in your business and rise as a person of influence, it will be easy to compare yourself to others questioniong what you're doing and your value. Understand though, that it's not about you. It's about God and the people you are meant to impact. The question, at the end of the day, is will people see more of you or more of Him?

Then, come back to the truth that you have been restored and made new in Christ.

3 Truths of Your Identify:

1. I am dearly loved for He delights in me (Colossians 3:12)
2. I am accepted (Ephesians 1:6)
3. I am complete (Colossians 2:10, John 1:16)

You are not your past, your fear, or your failure. You don't have to be perfect because God is perfecting you. "Take your joy from what God is doing in you, rather than from what you are doing for Him." (Wayne Cordeiro, author of *Jesus Pure & Simple*)

"Always come back to the truth that you have been restored and made new in Christ!"

Read

Deut. 7:6-8 | Isaiah 43: 18-19 | Colossians 3:12,
Ephesians 1:6 | Colossians 2:10 | John 1:16

Reflect

What lies about my identity have I been
believing?

_____

_____

_____

_____

_____

_____

_____

_____

Turn those lies into positive affirmations
and back them up with the truth
Scripture speaks over you.

_____

_____

_____

_____

_____

_____

_____

_____

_____

_____

PRAY

Praise | Repent | Ask | Yay

Father, keep me aware of your grace
and in awe of your love. Thank you for making
me new through you. Continue to lead me and
give me discernment as I grow my business and
lead new people you have assigned for me to
lead. Help me to walk boldly in faith and
freedom you have blessed me with and help me
to lovingly extend the same to others.

In Jesus name, Amen.

A Stewardship Heart

Day 6

"Each of you should use whatever gift you have received to serve others, as faithful stewards of God's grace in its various forms."
1 Peter 4:10

The dictionary defines the word steward as someone who "manages or looks after another's property." Have you ever thought of your gifts and talents as being property of God? When you think of it that way, it puts a whole new meaning to the saying "working for the Lord."

Everything you have been given is truly a gift from God. You are meant to be a good steward of your gifts and talents and use them to serve others.

How do you do this though?

You show up. You love yourself. You love people.

It's easy to overcomplicate serving the Lord. The world wants you to believe that you have to be the most popular or have millions of followers to be significant enough to serve. That just simply is not true. If you only have ten people following you, then that is still ten lives that you can positively impact.

> *"It's easy to overcomplicate serving the Lord. The thought that you need to be the most popular or have a massive following is simply not true."*

To have a steward's heart simply means that your heart's desires are guided by the Spirit. We are to be faithful and obedient by going where He leads even when it's scary or unfamiliar. We are here to love Jesus, abide in Him, be loved by Him, love others, and make disciples. Where you are can be your mission field. Let's put those gifts to work.

Read

1 Peter 4:10 | Exodus 23:25-26 | 1 Corinthians
2:16 | Luke 4:18 | Luke 16:11 | Genesis 1:28,

Colossians 3:23

Reflect

Where would you have me go, Lord?

_____

_____

_____

_____

_____

_____

What would you have me do, Lord?

_____

_____

_____

_____

_____

_____

What would you have me say, Lord,
and to whom?

_____

_____

_____

_____

_____

_____

PRAY

Praise | Repent | Ask | Yay

Father, thank you so much for the gifts and
talents you have given me. Forgive me if I have
not always been a good steward of them for your
kingdom. I want to serve you Lord. I want to do
your will and show up in the world for your kingdom. Show me how. Where should I show up?
Who should I show up for? Guide me Father. I
am your vessel. Use me. Thank you for those you
will bring into my life that I will get to serve with
the gifts and talents you have given me. Thank
you for blessing my business so that I can turn
around and bless more in the world.

In your name I pray, Amen.

You Are a Mighty Warrior

Day 7

"When the angel of the Lord appeared to Gideon, he said, 'The Lord is with you mighty warrior.'" - Judges 6:12

There are countless stories in the bible where God chooses what society would call the least of these, the most unexpected characters, or those who seem to be the most unqualified to step up and step in to their true identity that God places on them. For example, when we first meet Gideon, he is threshing wheat in a wine press to hide it from the Midianites. The angel of the Lord appears and calls Gideon "mighty warrior". In Gideon's eyes he was anything but a mighty warrior. In Judges 6:15, he describes himself as being the "least in my family." He was playing small and hiding the strength and potential God had placed inside of him. Gideon does not believe he is called to save his tribe and defeat the Midianites. He does not believe he is the right person for the job based on what society is telling him. He does not have the right background. He does not have the right qualifications. Who is he to lead an army and defeat the Midianites?

Have you felt God calling you, but you are shrinking back believing that you are unqualified, don't have the right look, or speak the right way? We know we have felt this way before. Gideon's story is to encourage the uncertain leader. It is God's prescence and His work on our behalf that we can conquer. You can be used if you are willing to believe and get moving in your calling.

"Before God's calling, He calls you 'mighty warrior'!"

The truth is, God gives you your identity. You are a mighty warrior. You have supernatural favor because you are the daughter of the true King. God puts desires on your heart because He is asking you to trust Him to provide. God does not need you to be the most qualified, the best dressed or have the biggest following. God provided all that Gideon needed to defeat the Midianites and in fact, he only used 300 soldiers to do it. Gideon was out numbered and all hope seemed lost, but with God all things are possible!

Read

Judges 6: 11-27

Reflect

What desires have been placed on my heart?
Discern between the desires of the flesh and
desires of the Spirit.

_____

_____

_____

_____

_____

_____

How can I lean in more to God's provision
for my business?

_____

_____

_____

_____

_____

What other adjectives can I use to describe
my identity as a daughter of a king?

_____

_____

_____

PRAY

Praise | Repent | Ask | Yay

Father, thank you for creating me to be your
daughter. Thank you for creating me to go out
and create a business with kingdom impact.
Father, I ask for your forgiveness for not
always trusting in you and your perfect plans
and timing for my life and business. I ask you to
open my ears and mind so that I may hear your
voice and gain wisdom for the guidance you are
providing for me. You know exactly who I need
to serve and how I need to serve them. Show me
your ways, Father. I praise your name for always
being there for me and never forsaking me. I
praise you for the abundance and victory you
provide for me when all hope seems lost.
In your name I pray, Amen.

Self Worth
& Value

Day 8

"Let each person examine his own work, and then he can take pride in himself alone, and not compare himself with someone else."
Galatians 6:4

D o you find days where you get caught up comparing yourself to others or maybe even trying to compete with where they are at or what they are doing? It's easy to look at what someone else has or where someone else is on the achievement scale and think, "I would love that," or "Why does it seem so easy for them?"

But we don't know that person's history. We don't see the work and their own personal struggles that probably went into them achieving success. One of our mentors always said, don't compare your chapter 1 to someone else's chapter 20.

Think about what Paul went through in order to advance the Kingdom of God. We know about Him today as one of the great apostles who helped transform thousands of lives. However, on that journey towards bearing much fruit, he was beaten, persecuted, imprisoned, mocked, and shipwrecked.

So on your way to pursuing your purpose and achieving greatness, there will be trials, lowlands and highlands; but God is faithful to complete the calling.

"Your worth is not defined by achievements ..."

He chose to create you in His image. You are a reflection of God's glory. That means you can reflect His character, love, patience, forgiveness, kindness, and faithfulness. Remember, there is only one YOU. You have a message and light that only YOU can share. No one else can do it like you can.

Your worth is not defined by possessions, achievements, physical attractiveness, or how many followers you have. Self Worth is not envying someone else. It is not criticizing or downgrading yourself.

Self worth is knowing you were created in His likeness. You can be confident in knowing you are a daughter of Christ, loved infinitely by Him, with gifts to share where you can make a valuable contribution to the lives of those around you.

"You can be confident knowing you are a daughter of Christ!"

Read

Galatians 6:4 | Genesis 1: 1-26

Reflect

Write down the negative thoughts or criticisms
you catch yourself saying about yourself.

_____

_____

_____

_____

_____

_____

_____

_____

_____

Now, cross them out and write positives
about yourself instead.

_____

_____

_____

_____

_____

_____

_____

_____

_____

_____

_____

PRAY

Praise | Repent | Ask | Yay

Lord, thank you for loving me so much that
you made me in your image. Thank you for even
knowing and caring about the number of hairs
on my head. I can't hardly even fathom your love
for me. I am so grateful that you chose me. Help
me to love myself, to be confident, and to trust
the path you're leading me on no matter how
difficult it can feel some days. Thank you for
being faithful and always fulfilling your
promises.

In Jesus name, Amen.

I Am the Proverbs 31 Woman

Day 9

"A woman who fears the Lord is to be praised."
Proverbs 31:30

I am a wife of noble character. I am worth far more than rubies. My husband has full confidence in me and I lack nothing of value.

I bring my husband good, not harm, all the days of my life.

I am an entrepreneur and work with eager hands. I am like the merchant ships bringing my products and services to customers all over the world.

I wake up every morning with a servant's heart ready to provide for my family and serve my customers and teammates.

I prayerfully consider my business decisions before I make them and the Lord blesses me with profits.
With my profits, I reinvest in my community and diversify my income.

I set about my work vigorously and my arms are strong for my tasks. My business is profitable. I am able to provide for my family with my earnings. I tithe ten percent to my church and extend my helping hands to those in need in my community.

"I wake up every morning with a servant's heart."

Regardless of the economy or the changing season, I do not fear for my business or my household. We are clothed in fine linen.

My husband is respected in our city. He is a leader in our community.

I continue to create and produce new products and services for my customers.

I am clothed with strength and dignity. I can laugh at

the days to come. I speak with wisdom and faithful instruction is on my tongue. I watch over the affairs of my household and do not eat the bread of idleness.

My children grow and call me blessed. My husband praises me.

Many women do noble things, but I surpass them all.

Charm is deceptive and beauty is fleeting, but because I fear the Lord, I am praised. I will give praise to the Lord for the many blessings I have been given.

"I am clothed with strength & dignity"

Read

Provers 31:10-31

Reflect

Recite this to yourself daily and step into your
identity as the Proverbs 31 woman. What
characteristics do you already have and can

celebrate?

_____

_____

_____

_____

Are there changes you need to make to become

more aligned with the Proverbs 31 woman?

_____

_____

_____

_____

_____

_____

_____

_____

_____

PRAY

Praise | Repent | Ask | Yay

Father, thank you for giving me a clear picture of what a woman after your heart in the business world looks like. Thank you for showing me that I am called to be a profitable entrepreneur while making a kingdom impact with my business at the same time. I ask for forgiveness for not always stepping into my calling and listening to your guiding whisper. I ask for you to give me wisdom and bring the right people into my business and repel those who are out to harm me. I celebrate the blessings you have given me through my business and the many more you are bringing my way. Help me to continue to grow successful so that I can turn around and use my blessings for the good of your kingdom.

In your name I pray, Amen.

Failure
Is Feedback

Day 10

"Rejoice always, pray continually, give thanks in all circumstances; for this is God's will."
1 Thessalonians 5:16-18

D o you ever just feel like a failure in your business? Have you ever asked yourself, "What am I doing?" Do you ever feel like you've failed so many times that you're ready to just quit?

I (Brandie) am right there with you sister. I have failed a lot. I've missed many goal deadlines. I've been discouraged, wanted to quit, and I wanted to just go back to my comfort zone. My type A Achiever cried many times because she hated missing deadlines and not hitting goals. Worst of all, when I missed these goals and felt like a failure, I was upset with God because I thought He should make it come easy and effortless. What I was doing was making accusations of the Lord and restricting Him to my timeline instead of waiting for Him.

Despite all the times I have failed, I have a proven track record of "failures" that have turned out to be blessings in disguise and turned into divinely orchestrated successes.

"Our 'failures' can turn into divinely orchestrated successes."

I realize though, that it doesn't stop the pain. It doesn't make the waiting any easier. However, it does leave me with a peace that surpasses understanding that God will work all things for my good according to *His* plan and purpose, not my own.

So what can we do today while we are in the pain and waiting?

1. We can say "Thank you"

Yep, show some gratitude for where you are today. You didn't just get to this point without some form of growth. Failure is feedback. Failure provides learning opportunities. So today, we reflect with gratitude at the progress we made and the lessons we have learned.

Philippians 4:6-7 - *"Do not be anxious about anything, but in every situation, by prayer and petition, with thanksgiving, present your requests to God, And the peace of God which transcends all understanding, will guard your heart and your minds."*

1 Thessalonians 5:16-18 - *"Rejoice always, pray continually, give thanks in all circumstancing; for this is God's will."*

Colossians 4:2 - *"Devote yourself to prayer, being watchful and thankful."*

2. Lean in

Lean in to God's whisper. He is not in the chaos or the noise, He is in the stillness. Go to a quiet space with a journal and pray, "What is my next step?" Then listen.

Matthew 7:7-8 - *"Ask, Seek, Knock."*

3. We Press on

Just because you don't hit your goal on your timeline doesn't mean you won't hit it. Again, this has been proven over and over to me. I do vision boards every year and there have been goals that took me multiple years before I achieved the goal. However, I never stopped pursuing that mielstone even though it may not have come on my timeline, I have hit every goal and it's always been better than I imagined when it did actually come.

Philippians 3:14 - *"I press on toward the goal for the prize of the upward call of God."*

You are strong through Christ. You are victorious. You have peace that surpasses understanding. You have divine discernment guiding you as you take the next step into your calling. You are not behind. You are exactly where you need to be. Work with an unshakeable soul as unto the Lord. As hearers and doers of the Word, you have the tools to activate His promises and become the radiant leader you are.

Read

Philippians 4:6-7 | 1 Thessalonians 5:16-18
Colossians 4:2 | Matthew 7:7-8, 16

Philippians 3:14

Reflect

Write the power verses can you can use to
remind you of your true identity.

_____

_____

_____

_____

_____

_____

_____

_____

_____

_____

_____

_____

_____

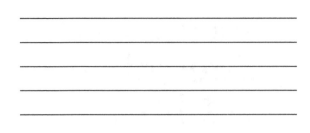

PRAY

Praise | Repent | Ask | Yay

Father, thank you for making me your daughter. Thank you for giving me this royalty status and holy spirit empowerment to step into my unique calling. I ask forgiveness for taking so long to answer your call or doubt that I was created for this moment in time. I ask for your confidence and discernment to come inside me and guide me as I take that next step. I praise your name over the people you will bring into my life, for the blessings to come, and those you will protect me from on this journey.

In your name I pray, Amen.

Renew Your Strength in Christ

Day 11

"He gives strength to the weary and increases the power of the weak." - Isaiah 40:29

There will be days along the journey where you will feel worn out, tired, weary, not sure if you even want to keep working on your business because of everything else going on around you. What we love is that even in the midst of changes around us, we can be reminded that God is the same today as He was yesterday, and He'll be the same tomorrow. He is our constant.

Do not feel like you have to do everything on your own. Share your worries and your weariness with Him because He is never too tired or too busy to listen. When you feel like life might be coming down around you, remember to ask Christ to renew your strength each day.

Also, go back to that notebook. You know the one tucked away in a drawer or bag somewhere. The one where you wrote down your vision and goals when you were so excited about the future. Go back and read that. Feel that feeling again-that excitement-that rush of

> *"Share your worries and your weariness with Him!"*

energy. Life may look a little different today, but may His word and your notebook remind you of where you're going and that you don't have to be in this alone.

It's okay if you need to slow down, rest, or step back for a minute. Re-evaluate where your energy should be. But don't forget you were meant to be a fearless influencer and world changer. Don't allow the circumstances of today take you away from the joys of tomorrow. Renew your strength in your creator.

Read

Isaiah 40:28-31 | Isaiah 41:10,13

Hebrews 13:8 | Philippians 4:13

Reflect

What is taking up a lot of your time and causing
stress or fear? Write those things down. Then
release them up to Him.

_____

_____

_____

_____

_____

_____

_____

_____

What is one thing you can commit to doing each
day to make sure you are being renewed in Him?

_____

_____

_____

_____

_____

_____

PRAY

Praise | Repent | Ask | Yay

Father, thank you for reminding me of your constant source of strength and comfort. Thank you for always being with me and giving your gift of peace. I know I have days where I try to do everything on my own. I try to be in control and not ask for help which causes me to get burned out. So I ask that you restore my strength and trust in you so that I build my life and business with you at the center. I know you will direct my steps, and I can find comfort in knowing that with you all things are possible. Give me courage, strength, and hope in You as I move forward no matter what is happening in my life. Thank you for the blessing of knowing you, Lord. In Jesus name, Amen.

Releasing Control

Day 12

"Commit your work to the Lord and your plans will succeed." - Proverbs 16:3

W e often hear the phrase, "failing to plan is planning to fail." To some extent this is true. If you don't have plans or create a vision, then it's easy to stay stuck or complacent with where life is. It's important to take action steps each day.

However, don't be so tied to those plans that when things don't go accordingly, it causes you to break down, feel discouraged, and get too much in your head. Sometimes we can be so caught up in our ambition that we lose sight of the calling God has us in now.

If you become too preoccupied with planning and wanting everything to go smoothly, then those plans become an idol, and you fail to allow room for God to make moves in your life and business.

Proverbs 19:21 says, "You can make many plans, but the Lord's purpose will prevail." Are you open to God shifting your plans and desires or prolonging them?

There were times when we saw our dreams being delayed, or when we realized we had to pivot in our business. What we thought we once wanted, God started shifting our hearts towards other paths where

> *"When you let Him do the leading, you will find empowerment."*

we could continue to be fruitful and multiply. That's what happens as you grow closer to Him and learn to release because of your trust. Jesus is like your soulmate. He has your best interest at heart. As you abide in Him, His desires will become your desires so you don't have to worry about making the wrong decision. You will know.

It's not easy to let go and release control, but Jesus died

to set you FREE! Keep your eyes on Him, no matter the circumstance. Let Him do the leading, and you will find empowerment with a life of abundance.

He won't lead you onto a new path or to complete a new task without equipping you with the tools to do it.

If all you do is seek your will and try to stick to your plan, you will find yourself discouraged and burned out from all the striving.

So we must seek His will. God's timing, especially His delays, can feel like He isn't answering, but we have personally experienced several times throughout our journey that God's will and timing has always been perfect.

He will meet all your needs according to His perfect schedule and purpose for your life. Patiently release control and await His timing.

*"God's will and timing
are always perfect!"*

Read

Proverbs 16:3 | Proverbs 19:21 | John 11:1-45
Philippians 2:3-4 | Jeremiah 29:11

Hebrews 13:20-21 | Proverbs 3:5-6

Reflect

In what areas do you feel like you have to be in
control and struggle to be flexible
with your plans?

_____

_____

_____

_____

_____

_____

Spend time in prayer releasing that control and
those plans to Him. Turn on some worship
music, pray over those plans, pray for
discernment to know when to make shifts.

_____

_____

Are there areas where you have found yourself working out of selfish ambition?

_____

_____

_____

_____

_____

PRAY

Praise | Repent | Ask | Yay

Father, thank you for your love and wanting to do life with me. I praise you for always watching over me and for your promise to give me a future and a hope. Show me any areas where I work or plan out of selfish ambition. Help me, Father, to come from a place of love and a heart of generosity. I want to know your will, and I trust in you. Continue to lead me and speak to me as I spend time in your presence. Give me the strength to release control or any anxieties to you. Thank you for not leaving me to walk this journey alone. Lead me and I will follow.

In your name, Amen

Finding Rest in Him

Day 13

"Very early in the morning, while it was still dark, Jesus got up, left the house and went off to a solitary place, where he prayed."
Mark 1:35

It can be easy to fill your day up from morning 'til night or to even have all the time in the world, and not take the time to rest in Him. Sometimes we get so busy doing things for our kids, our spouses, our jobs, and trying to hit goals for our business that we put ourselves and even our relationship with God on the back burner. Before you know it, you can end up feeling burnt out and unfulfilled. Right back to where you might have felt at the beginning when starting your business. We must remember that none of what we do and or are working towards will mean anything if we are not doing it alongside Him. We must follow in Jesus' footsteps. Even He made being still a priority.

When Jesus felt stressed, worried, worn out, or just needed to gather his thoughts, he got alone with God. In Mark Chapter 1, we see where Jesus spends a long day healing the sick and casting out demons. Then in verse 35, we see that Jesus wakes up early before anyone else and goes out to pray.

I (Natalie) don't know about you, but I've definitely never been a morning person; however when I need to wake up at 3:30 to catch a plane for vacation, I have no problem doing that. So that tells me no matter what's going on in my day, I need to make Him a priority.

"I need to make time with Jesus a priority first thing each morning!"

Jesus took time to pray. This is a vital link between you and God. Like Jesus, we must find time away from others to spend time with God and feed our Spirit. I found using a prayer journal allows me to get my thoughts out without distractions.

We believe God gives us an assignment and work to do while here, but it doesn't mean we have to strive and be in lack to complete it. Stop trying to make it all happen. Stop trying for perfection. Simply abide in Him. Your wisdom, renewal, and your strength will come from resting in your spirit.

So be careful not to run your day and business like the world, where you feel like you always have to be in hustle mode to get anything accomplished. Jesus wants to walk with you, so be willing to kick off those running shoes as to not run ahead of Him. We never want to be so consumed by our daily tasks that we don't make time for our Savior and miss hearing His voice.

In Him is where you will find peace, refuge, knowledge, love, and all He promises in Matthew 11:28-30: *"Come to me all you who are weary and carry heavy burdens, an I will give you rest. Take my yoke upon you. Let me teach you, because I am humble and gentle, and you will find rest for your souls. For my yoke fits perfectly, and the burden I give you is light."*

Don't you feel uplifted already just by reading that!? So go and bask in His unfailing love.

"Jesus wants to walk with us; we have to be willing to kick off those running shoes!"

Read

Jeremiah 9: 23-24 | 1 Thess. 5:16-18 | Mark 1:35

Mark 6:45-46 | Luke 5:16 | Matthew 6:33

Reflect

When will you commit to getting alone with God
daily? Write that in your calendar and set your
alarm. Make this your #1 daily nonnegotiable for
your life and business.

_____

_____

_____

_____

_____

_____

_____

You can refer to our Mindful Morning routine to
help you get going and find what works for you.
List some you can implement to get the most out
of your alone time with Him.

_____

_____

_____

_____

_____

_____

PRAY

Praise | Repent | Ask | Yay

Father, you are my rock. I will praise you, my God and King. You Lord are my loving ally and my fortress. I praise you for your unfailing love.

I'm sorry that there are times when I do everything else in a day except spend time alone with you. I know that sometimes my time spent with you is only on the way to work or while getting myself ready. But Jesus, I want more of you. Teach me and help me to be still in your presence. Help me to listen, be mindful, and be prayerful. Father, I want to seek you first. Thank you for showing us that it's good to rest and be with you. I know I will be better because of it. Remind me that moments spent seeking you will never return void. I find hope in you!

In Jesus name, Amen.

The Core Values of Success

Day 14

"If you belonged to the world, it would love you as its own. As it is, you do not belong to the world, but I have chosen you out of the world." John 15:19

I (Brandie) have been caught up in what the world's definition of success seems to be or at least my perception of what that definition is. In the past, I have measured my value against its definition that I have to have a certain number in my bank account, drive a certain type of car, wear certain clothes, have a certain education, and the list can go on. Don't get me wrong, I love having money in my bank account, wearing nice clothes, driving a nice car, and having a good education. These things are great, and I truly want each of you to experience these blessings.

But am I not successful if I don't have all or some of those things? The enemy tries to convince us to be of the world instead of in the world. He will try to get you to believe the story that if you don't have a specific number in your bank account that you're not successful or worthy or bring value. That's why it's so important to question the stories in our minds and where we place our value.

When we start questioning the stories of what success looks like and how we can have a successful life, we can go back to the powerful example in the Proverbs 31 woman.

Proverbs 31
Characteristics of a Successful Woman:

1. Success in Character = Noble Character, worth more than rubies.

2. Success in marriage = Husband is confident in her and lacks nothing of value.

3. Success in health and Physically fit = works with eager hands, works vigorously, arms are strong for her tasks.

4. Success in family/home = provides and takes care of her family, her children call her blessed, clothed in scarlet, lamp does not go out at night, fine linen.

5. Success socially = provides portions for her servants (employees), gives to the needy.

6. Successful in business = profitable trades, considers her investments (makes smart business decisions and reinvests earnings into multiple streams of income).

7. Clothed with strength and dignity = laughs, wise, speaks truth.

8. Fears the Lord = woman who fears the Lord is to be praised and given the reward she has earned.

Through it all, let's not be anxious about anything for as we know the Lord your God will go with you where you go. God doesn't have small things in store for you. Recognize your need for Him, but know you are set apart. Keep moving in your vision and live a life worthy of your calling.

*"We are IN this world,
but not OF this world."*

Read

Proverbs 31: 10 - 31 | Proverbs 3:1-5 | 1Kings 2:3

Reflect

Where are you successful based on what
scripture tells us?

_____

_____

_____

_____

_____

_____

_____

In which of your core values; health, family,
finances, business...can you implement healthy
success habits?

_____

_____

_____

_____

_____

_____

_____

_____

_____

PRAY

Praise | Repent | Ask | Yay

Father, thank you for showing me an example of what your definition of success can look like for a woman. You created me to be healthy, happy, and abundant in all areas of my life, not just in my business. Forgive me for not always having my priorities straight and for getting my core values out of alignment with your wants for my life. I ask you to reveal to me any areas of my life where I am not living up to my full potential and to show me how I can get back in alignment with your vision and path for my life. Thank you for creating me to be a woman of strength and dignity who is able to laugh without fear of the future because I know you are already going ahead to work all things for my good.

Thank you Jesus. Amen.

Success
(In God's Eyes)

Day 15

"Now I commit you to God and to the word of his grace, which can build you up and give you an inheritance among all those who are sanctified." - Acts 20:32

On this journey of Rising to Your Purpose, you will also be seeking success. In order to live well, live humbly, and live in fulfillment, you need to be able to identify what success means to you. Oftentimes, we can get caught up in chasing success or the feeling of it. When we don't hit a goal, it's easy to feel discouraged. It's easy to feel that life is a failure unless you're getting something out of it; glory, fun, money, popularity. But Paul thought life was worth nothing unless he used it for God's glory and work.

That's where the mindset shift needs to happen; from focusing on ourselves and what we want, to seeking

God's will and how we can do His work for His glory. Paul believed what he put into life was far more important than what he got out of it.

"My life is worth nothing unless I use it for doing the work assigned me by the Lord Jesus." Acts 20:24

We also go on to read that Paul was satisfied with whatever he had and was given. So as you work to grow our business and gain wealth, evaluate also what wealth means to you and your attitude towards wealth and comfort. If you focus more on what you don't have,

"Focus on the gifts God has given you and put His work back in first place!"

you will come up short every time. Instead focus on the gifts God has given you and put God's work back in first place. Find the miracles and blessings in each new day.

We can also learn from the prophet Jeremiah, who worked wholeheartedly to try and help restore the nation, but most people and religious leaders wouldn't listen to Him. In the world's eyes, at the time, he didn't look, feel, or act successful. He had no money, family, or friends. Yet, here we are, reading about him today and how God was able to use him. We are able to see that Jeremiah successfully completed the work God gave him to do.

That is where you can also evaluate. Do you know your calling/mission? Are you being faithful to complete it regardless of what others think, say, or feel about it. God measures our success not by fame, fortune, and prosperity, but by obedience, faithfulness, discipline, and righteousness. If you are faithfully doing the work God has given you, you are successful in His eyes.

"Do we know our assignment and are we being faithful to complete it?"

Read

Acts 20: 32-35 | Jeremiah 1:1-8
Jeremiah 29:11 | Jeremiah 52

Reflect

Where are your priorities?

(For Deeper reflection see Haggai Chapters 1-2)

_____

_____

_____

_____

_____

_____

_____

_____

What does success mean to you?

Do you need to shift your focus?

_____

_____

_____

_____

_____

PRAY

Praise | Repent | Ask | Yay

Father, thank you for knowing me and loving
me just as I am. Thank you for forming me and
choosing me to do your work. Lord sometimes
I worry too much about what others think and
worry about having enough money and time to
do the things I want to do. Help me to
remember that it's not about me. It's about
you and growing your Kingdom. Help me to be
faithful, humble, and give me the endurance to
complete the work you give me. Remind me
daily to know my worth is not what the world
thinks of me, but Lord that I am your
daughter, may my worth and success be found in
you. Let that satisfy me. I want to serve you and
know you. Thank you for the love, discernment,
and prosperity you are bringing me as I delight
myself in you.

In Jesus name, Amen.

Be Still
& Attentive

Day 16

*"He says, 'Be still, and know that
I am God ...'"* - Psalm 46:10

T his is a check in. How is your quiet time going?
Do you plan your day with intentions of spending
time with the Lord, but then you oversleep or things
unexpected happen in your day? Next thing you know,
you've almost forgotten about spending time with Him.
You start to feel guilty about letting everything else
come first.

The next morning comes and you're on top of it. You're
up out of bed and you're creating space and room for
time alone with God, but all that's going on in the back
of your mind are other things you need to get done.
So then, you have a sense of guilt for not working on
things that need to be done around the house or for
your business.

What's a girl to do? First things first. RELEASE the guilt. "There is therefore now no shame or condemnation."

It's not ncessarily the time of day that matters, it's your closeness in thought, speech, actions, and spirit with Him. Jesus says we must draw near to Him. He is our Father. Just as you want to spend quality time with your children or significant other, God yearns for that quality time with you. The thing that pleases God is when you come to Him throughout your day recognizing your need for Him.

"The thing that pleases God most is seeking Him first!"

You will never be in control of all that's going on around you, so surrender to Him, relax, and let Him control the outcomes.

Continue to prioritize God and sit at the feet of Jesus every day asking the spirit to reframe and renew your mind. As you transform internally, you will see transformation in each area of life. "Be still and know." Activate the fullness of who you are in Christ.

Read

Matthew 6:33 | Psalm 46:10 | 1 Timothy 6:6-12

James 4:8 | Psalm 119:47-48

Reflect

Are you consistent in your alone time with God?

_____

_____

_____

_____

_____

_____

_____

How do you feel when spending time with Him,
or when choosing to do other things instead?
Surrender those feelings to Jesus and let time
with God be a non-negotiable in your day to day.

_____

_____

_____

_____

_____

_____

_____

_____

_____

_____

_____

PRAY

Praise | Repent | Ask | Yay

Father, I adore you. I praise you and the heaven
you are preparing for me. I want to know you
deeply. I desire to know you. But Lord I know I
get distracted and put things before you. Please
forgive me and provide me with the spiritual
strength and yearning to make you my number
1 priority. Strip me of any guilt I feel for when
making time to spend with you. I know it will
take creating habits where I look forward to that
time with you daily. Thank you Lord for
providing for me and all that you're granting me.
In Jesus name, Amen.

Boast About
My Weakness

Day 17

*"Jesus said, 'My grace is sufficient for you, for
my power is made perfect in weakness.'
Therefore, I will boast all the more
gladly about my weaknesses so that
Christ's power may rest on me."*
2 Corinthians 12:9

J esus is asking me to "boast about my weaknesses"...
Wait what!? It seems like everywhere I look,
people are sharing about their successes and
showcasing their highlight reel. It feels like, we should
hide our ugly imperfections, act tough, strive and
hustle to the top. Showing weakness is not allowed.
How can this be then, that Paul is telling us to be proud
and boast about our weaknesses? It does not make
sense.

Or does it?

Jesus tells us that His grace is sufficient for you. He says His power is made perfect in your weakness. You are enough because His grace makes you enough. You are powerful because He rests His power on you. You are more powerful in your weakness because you are using God's power and not your own strength to be victorious and rise.

You don't have to strive to be perfect or be ashamed of your imperfections because Jesus gives you grace to not strive and says your weakness and vulnerability is beautiful. Let this sink into your heart today.

"You are more powerful in your weakness because you are using God's power and not your own strength."

This is also where magnetic marketing kicks in. When we can be our authentic selves which includes vulnerability, that's when we can make genuine connections and truly impact. The beauty is, since we were given the free gift of Jesus with His death on the cross, we no longer have to strive or to earn. Simply be.

Read

2 Corinthians 12:9 | Galatians 3

Galatians 4:8-10

Reflect

How can you boast about your weaknesses?

_____

_____

_____

_____

_____

_____

_____

_____

_____

In what areas do you need to open up and be
vulnerable to allow God's power and glory
to shine through in your life?

_____

_____

PRAY

Praise | Repent | Ask | Yay

Father, thank you so much for being a living
God that speaks to me daily. You continuously
are breathing life into me through your word.
Thank you for that! I ask your forgiveness for
trying to be sufficient on my own without you
and your power and grace. I ask you to reveal to
me where I can boast about my weaknesses so
that your power may rest on me and your glory
can shine through. Thank you for turning all
things for my good. Even what I perceive to be
weaknesses you turn into my strength.

Amen.

You Will
be Tested in
the Wilderness

Day 18

*"Jesus, full of the Holy Spirit, left the
Jordan and was led by the Spirit into the
wilderness, where for forty days he was
tempted by the devil." - Matthew 4:1-2*

H ave you noticed that when you are trying to
change a habit, reprogram your mind, uplevel in
your business, or basically do anything that is making
you become a better version of yourself, you always go
through a season of being tested?

In Matthew chapter 4, we see that even Jesus was
tested by Satan in order to see if Jesus would stay
committed to what He was set out to do while on this

Earth. Just like Jesus was tested, you will be tested especially when doing work for the Kingdom.

In these moments of being tested, you have two options. You can either keep going, even when you fall or stumble, and continue to pursue your commitment, or you can give up and go back to your old ways of acting, thinking, being.

"You will be tested to see if you will actually do what you say you're going to do."

Which options will you choose when the season of testing is upon you?

Will you stand firm in your belief in who God says He is?

If you begin to doubt if your calling is still the direction you should go, you can ask yourself these three questions:

1. Does it light me up?

2. Is it good for me and others around me?

3. Does it allow me to create impact?

Just because you're being tested, does not mean you have to stand down and not fight back when you're on your journey to Kingdom impact. You don't have to tolerate the enemy messing with you. This is where your power verses come into play. Fight back with scripture just as Jesus did.

Every time you speak God's word, you are activating the scriptures. You already have the power within you through the Holy Spirit and you have the tools through the Bible. It's time for you to claim your victory!

*"When you are being
tempted, fight back
with Scripture!"*

Read

Matthew 4: 1-11 | Ephesians 6:10-20

Reflect

What are your power verses of defense?

_____

_____

_____

_____

_____

_____

_____

_____

How are you feeling about your calling? What
might be your next steps?

_____

_____

_____

_____

_____

_____

PRAY

Praise | Repent | Ask | Yay

Father, I thank you for always being there waiting to build and grow a relationship with me. Please forgive me for not always showing up for our one on one time and for putting other tasks over you as a priority. I ask for you to give me the strength to break free from the enemy's distractions throughout the day and always come back to you for my source of strength, hope, peace and truth. You are my all in all and everything I need to be fulfilled.

In your name I pray, Amen.

Boundaries
Are a Blessing
Day 19

"Jesus was inside the boat, sleeping with his head on a pillow ..." - Mark 4:38

How many times have you said yes to something and then regretted it later? Have you ever bent over backwards for others only to be left feeling unappreciated and completely drained? How many times have you needed to rest, but instead you poured so much of yourself out that at the end of the day you were left feeling burnt out, resentful, and empty?

If you are reading this and shaking your head yes and recalling all of the times you've felt drained, resentful, unappreciated, burnt out, and completely empty; then it's time for you to start setting boundaries in your life and business and actually keep them!

Sister, boundaries are healthy. Boundaries are necessary if you want to build a sustainable business and a healthy synergistic life for yourself and your family. We know that setting boundaries are important because Jesus set boundaries!

Throughout Scripture, you repeatedly see Jesus saying no to things or people that would be harmful to Him or His purpose. He rested and observed quiet time alone, ate healthy, was active, and required others to do their part before giving them a miracle. Because Jesus set boundaries, He was able to not fall into the burnout

"Boundaries are healthy, and they're necessary!"

trap. Instead He received the fullness of God so that His cup ran over. Jesus also consistently took time to come back to God and spend time with Him. He did not rely on his own strength.

Jesus' examples throughout scripture remind us that if we want to fulfill our purposes in life and be blessings to others, we must set healthy boundaries.

It is not selfish. In order to serve and love others wholeheartedly, they need you to first take care of yourself. The more love you pour into yourself, the more love that will overflow in abundance and spread to those around you.

"To serve and love others wholeheartedly, they need you to first take care of yourself!"

Read

Mark 4:38 | Luke 7:36 | John 10:39 - 40

Reflect

What is causing you to feel stressed, frustrated,
or resentful?

_____

_____

_____

_____

_____

_____

_____

_____

_____

What areas of your life do you need to
set boundaries?

_____

_____

PRAY

Praise | Repent | Ask | Yay

Jesus, thank you for teaching me what setting
healthy boundaries can look like in my life.
Please forgive me for not always keeping my
commitments to you and my body which is a
temple you gave me to care for. I ask you to give
me wisdom to see where I need to set
boundaries in the different areas of my life and
the strength to keep those commitments to
myself and communicate them effectively to
those that may need to keep them as well. I
praise you for always loving me and showing me
grace.

In your name I pray, Amen.

Walking
In Obedience

Day 20

"'Martha, Martha,' the Lord answered, 'you are worried and upset about many things, but few things are needed—or indeed only one. Mary has chosen what is better, and it will not be taken away from her.'"
Luke 10:41-42

Obedience. As independent women, this can be one of the hardest things to live out. It's easy for us to want to seek control, have everything planned out, and live life on our terms. Isn't that what we see everywhere, "Live life on your terms." However, as Christian women and entrepreneurs, we truly need to be seeking the Lord's will and living life on His terms out of obedience to what He has for us.

It takes courage to act in obedience because sometimes we have a desire in our heart, but God is also revealing a different direction for us. Therefore, again we must discern whether the desire is of the flesh or of the Spirit.

The world and social media can make so many things look and sound good. It's tempting to have shiny object syndrome and feel like we have to build our business a certain way or we can't be successful. However, God might be calling you to do business and life differently than what is paraded in front of you.

> *"God might be calling you to do business and life differently."*

He might be calling you to be present in your season of life, to slow down, to not worry about how much you are posting or how many likes you have.

Instead of striving and yearning for more followers or more money, yearn for more intimacy with Jesus. Then, allow the Lord to reveal to you what you should do, how you should build, with whom you should work with.

We can't worry about the timing or the money.

Determine what is God's priority for you in your life right now and get busy pouring into those areas.

Some will be called to pour more time into the family and relationships they have. Others may be called to pour more into their business. Some may be called to both.

Regardless, don't compare yourself to where others are saying you should be or what you should do. Where does God say you should be right now?

Where He calls, will you walk in obedience as Peter, Andrew, James, and John did? (Matthew 4:18-22)

When we seek God first (Matthew 6:33) everything we really need will fall into place.

Ask God for wisdom and knowledge as King Solomon did. Don't be afraid to seek wise Godly counsel either. See what God blesses you with from first seeking Him and His wisdom. (2 Chronicles 1:1-13)

"Don't compare yourself to where others are saying you shold be or what you should do."

Read

Mark 4:13-20 | 2 Chronicles 1-4
Matthew 4:18-22 | Jeremiah 38
1 Kings 17:13-16 | 1 John 2: 15-17
Romans 12:2 | Deuteronomy 30:9

Reflect

Where is God calling you to pour into right
now and how does that look?

_____

_____

_____

_____

_____

Praise God for all he has done for you, and
ask Him for wisdom in this season.

_____

_____

_____

_____

What does walking in obedience mean to you?

_____

_____

_____

_____

PRAY

Praise | Repent | Ask | Yay

Lord, I sit here in reverence and in awe of you,
your life, your favor, and your miracles. I see
how you're molding me and teaching me. Thank
you for family, mentors, relationships in my
life, and for all the resources to help me grow.
Father forgive me when I try to take control and
do things my way in my will. I want my will to
be yours. Align my heart and desires with yours
Father. I want to be kingdom driven and not get
caught up in the things of this world. Grant me
wisdom, knowledge, and supernatural power to
walk humbly, courageously, willingly, and obe-
diently in your will. Thank you for entrusting me
to share your love with others.
In Jesus name, Amen.

Authentic Leadership

Day 21

*"He chose you in advance and He makes
everything work out according to His plan."*
Ephesians 1:11

There will be times when you don't feel equipped or
you will worry if you are doing enough. Therefore,
remember the scripture above. When these times
come, take time to reflect and evaluate your actions.
Are you leading the best you know how to? Are you
continuously working on your own personal and
leadership development? Are you showing compassion
and love for others as Jesus did? Are you reflecting
Christ and letting His light shine through you?

Remember you have been chosen and in many ways,
like Esther, for such a time as this.

Are we each going to lead the same way? No. This is
where you get to put your own spin on how you run

your business, your group, and organization. This is how you begin stepping into an authentic leader.

There will also be times when you might sit and worry if you are being heard or noticed and wonder if anyone cares? It's hard to keep doing the work without any recognition.

Remember Jesus didn't always receive the recognition He deserved either while serving. It's not about you.

"Remember, you have been chosen ... for such a time as this!"

Yes these are real feelings that we can all experience from time to time but Paul reminds us in Galatians 6:9 , "Let us not grow weary in doing good."

Feelings rarely make a good compass and there will be times where you just don't feel like doing anything or working with a teammate is difficult.

Be careful as you step into leadership to not seek the approval of man more than you seek the approval of God.

Your desire for approval is a craving that others can never satisfy. What you really need to crave is increased intimacy with Jesus.

As you continue to build and rise as a leader, use the truth as your anchor and not do things just to get more followers and likes. Work on keeping your motives pure and in alignment with your mission.

"As you contine to rise as a leader, use the truth as your anchor and work on keeping your motives pure and mission-aligned!"

Read

Ephesians 1:11 | Galatians 6:9 | Matthew 20:26
Ecclesiastes 9:10 | Philippians 2:3-4

Reflect

What is the next thing you can do to grow in
your development as an authentic leader?

_____

_____

_____

_____

_____

_____

_____

_____

_____

_____

How can you reflect the character of Christ in
your life and business?

_____

_____

_____

_____

_____

_____

_____

_____

_____

PRAY

Praise | Repent | Ask | Yay

Jesus, I want my life and leadership to flow
from my relationship with You. I want to share
with others the life and love that you have given
me. Help me to stay steadfast in your word to lay
a solid foundation in order to lead others. Thank
you for loving me and choosing me.

In your name, Amen.

Working With
A Pure Heart
Day 22

*"Create in me a pure heart, O God, and
renew a steadfast spirit within me."
Psalm 51:10*

This is the prayer of David to God after he
committed adultery with Bethesda. He knew what
he did was wrong and he pleaded with God for
forgiveness and for his heart to be renewed. The
desires of the flesh can overcome the desires of the
Spirit. Jesus even warns his disciples in Matthew 26:41
to be on guard against temptation as the Spirit is
willing but the flesh is weak.

Have you ever prayed like David over your
entrepreneurial heart and Spirit? Have you ever been
tempted to do something that maybe was unethical or
out of alignment with your values? It can be difficult
to keep a pure heart when you are building a business.

There are so many ways, if not careful, that your heart can turn its focus from serving the Spirit to serving the flesh. It is easy to get caught up in the world's definition of success and expectations for achievement. You find yourself craving the accolades and thirst for significance.

If you are not hitting a certain rank, promotion, or financial goal then you feel worthless. Maybe you even

"There are so many ways our hearts can turn their foucs from serving the Spirit to serving the flesh."

begin to make decisions to behave in the gray area that deep down you know are not right. You lose sight of what is in alignment with the God given purpose for your business and why you started it to begin with. You put your success in one defined end result that was set by the world's standards instead of the souls and lives you have changed in the process of going after those results.

Having monetary success and receiving accolades and recognition are not bad things to have and experience. None of that is wrong. These things of the world only become hindering when the accolades and money are all that you are chasing. It is dangerous when those are the only way you define your self worth.

God put you in the entrepreneurial space for a reason. He created desires in your heart to serve the world with your services and products. You are exactly where you are meant to be. God wants you to thrive and live a victorious life, but he wants you to have a heart for His people. He calls you to show up in this economy as a light for His Kingdom. Chasing the ways of the world will leave you in the grind and unfulfilled. Chasing God's desires for you and your business will leave you with a pure heart and steadfast Spirit that will be able to thrive on your journey to your God sized dream.

"Chasing God's desires for you and your business will leave you with a pure heart!"

Read

Psalm 51:10 | Matthew 26:41

Reflect

Are there unhealthy ties in your business
that you need to cut off?

_____

_____

_____

_____

_____

_____

_____

_____

_____

Are you feeling out of alignment with clients,
activities, or strategies that you need to
adjust to get back in alignment?

_____

_____

_____

_____

_____

_____

_____

_____

_____

PRAY

Praise | Repent | Ask | Yay

Father, thank you for the desires you have put in
my heart. Forgive me for not always
following your desires and for sometimes putting
my wants and needs over what you have called
me to do with my business. I ask that you create
in me a clean heart and purify me of unhealthy
desires. I want to know your will and to live it
out in my life. Let me be a light for you and your
kingdom. I know you are creating a future more
beautiful and victorious than I could ever
imagine. You are working all things
for my good. I praise your name!
Amen

Letting Go
Day 23

"Forget the former things; do not dwell on the past. See, I am doing a new thing! Now it springs up; do you not perceive it? I am making a way in the wilderness and streams in the wasteland."
Isaiah 43: 18-19

Sometimes to go to the next level, we have to be willing to let go. We have to let go of possessions, past dreams that maybe aren't a part of us any longer, past relationships that no longer serve us, and that which we cannot control. In order to move forward with God as our CEO, we have to be willing to surrender.

There's a quote from Natasha Hazlett in her book, *Unstoppable Influence*, that says, "Maybe the journey isn't so much about becoming anything. Maybe it's about un-becoming everything that isn't really you, so you can be who you were meant to be in the first place."

We have to allow our minds and body to relax, especially as high achievers and women of empath. We cannot build capacity for more on our own.

Is God steering you in a new direction; an unknown that is a little frightening because you lack control of the outcome?

That thought alone can make us anxious and uneasy.

> *"In order to move forward with God as our CEO, we must be willing to surrender."*

But when you understand and know that God's will and planning is always better than your own, you know what's on the other side will be worth it. Natasha goes on to write, "When you let things go that you cannot control and allow God to lead, you are able to open your world to more miracles, beauty, and abundance." God is abundant. He will not run out of resources for you. What do you want? Are you willing to do the work? Are you willing to go for it?

He's given you all that you need within, will bring you the tools and surround you with the right people. That's why you're reading this now.

So, what's that action you've been wanting to take? The one you've been thinking of every day, but it makes you scared to do it. Pray about it and ask God to grant you peace and to bless your decision. Remember you are One with Christ. Stand firm in your authority. Then take action.

"God's abundance will never run out of resources for you!"

Read

Isaiah 43:18-19 | Psalm 36: 7-9 | Ezekiel 36:26
Psalm 3:3-4 | Psalm 4:3

Reflect

What is that thing you've been holding back on,
but God is calling you to step out and step up?

_____

_____

_____

_____

_____

_____

_____

_____

_____

What do you need to let go of or un-become
in order to propel forward?

_____

_____

PRAY

Praise | Repent | Ask | Yay

Lord, I am grateful for the gifts you have in store for me. Sometimes I try to move too fast or too slow thinking things will happen in my timing, but I know your divine timing is perfect. You have given me what I already need. Help me to unleash my gifts and move boldly in faith. May all that I do and say glorify you. Thank you for speaking to me and for the discernment that comes with each passing day spent in your presence.

Amen

Moving Out Of Complacency

Day 24

"A sluggard's appetite is never filled, but the desires of the diligent are fully satisfied."
Proverbs 13:4

Today, I'm calling you to move out of complacency and out of your comfort zone. I know it feels safe and snuggly like sitting on the couch under a pile of blankets, but that sister, will not get you to where the Lord wants to plant you.

People like Rockefeller, Madam CJ Walker, Ford, or Network Marketing leaders like Kimberly Olson, Michelle Schaffer, Frazier Brooks, and Ray Higdon didn't create legacies by playing small and scared. Sure there were natural fears, but they moved forward despite them and weren't going to let anything or anyone hold them back from rising to their purpose.

Imagine what would have happened if Moses would

have stayed in Pharaoh's palace where it was easy and materialistically he had everything he could ever want or need. What if Esther would have hidden herself and not spoken up to the King? Ruth could have gone back home where the food was plenty and found comfort with a new husband there. Mary could have not said "Yes" to the calling on her life. Where would we be then? Now, I'm sure God would have found someone else to carry our Savior, but He chose Mary first.

"Take faith filled action He's got you!"

Just like He is choosing you. Yes, the road ahead might look a little intimidating. The outcome is most likely uncertain. That is why we don't walk the road alone. We abide in Jesus-our Savior, our leader, our friend.

So today, I want you to find your boldness and confidence in the truth, in the promises of God, and in His everlasting word.

Take some time today to meditate over these scriptures. Then get moving and take faith filled action forward. He's got you!

Read

Proverbs 13:4 | Psalm 84:11-12 | Psalm 85
Exodus 14:13-14 | 1 Chronicles 28:9
2 Chronicles 16:9 | Psalm 34:1-10
Proverbs 3:5-9 | Proverbs 13:13
Matthew 2:13-15 | Deuteronomy 1:19-26

Reflect

Take at least one of the verses from above and
write it down. Place it in a spot you will see
everyday to inspire you to take action even when
you aren't feeling like it.

_____

_____

_____

_____

_____

_____

What's been on your heart you feel God's asking
you to do? Do you need a mentor, do you need
to invest in training, do you need to participate
more in your team? Do you need to go live?...
What's the next step you can take?

PRAY

Praise | Repent | Ask | Yay

Father, my creator, my source of strength,
giver of all things. You are my light and my
protector. I know I have not been showing up
as confidently as I can or want to. I know that
I have been holding back. Forgive me for not
showing up to serve in the way that you have
called me to as a Christian entrepreneur. I am
boldly asking you to give me strength, give me
that confident mindset and spirit. I pray that I
listen to my spirit as you lead me.

Thank you for calling me.

In Jesus name, Amen

It Is By Faith

Day 25

"For we live by faith, not by sight."
2 Corinthians 5:7

I (Natalie) was watching the behind the scenes of the movie, *The New World,* with my husband. One of the actors spoke about how incredible it is to see how far America has come from the day the first of many colonists arrived up to present day. These colonists literally went into the unknown and risked everything for freedom and exploration.

Even with all the uncertainty and obstacles lying ahead, they still moved forward.

It got me thinking about our businesses and our spiritual journey. How far are we willing to travel into the unknown? How much do we hold back because we are afraid of what we don't know and the uncertainty. We think we need to have all the answers given to us before we make decisions, but if we are truly living by faith, we don't need all the answers. Faith comes by hearing the Word. Then, with total belief, we will manifest the blessings in our life.

Remember the bleeding woman? She heard about Jesus and what he was capable of doing. Her belief was so strong that she knew she would be healed if only she could touch His garment. Jesus felt the power leave him, because her faith was so strong.

"Faith is the confident assurance that what we hope for is going to happen."

She didn't question it. Belief without doubting is when we see the miracles.

We also see this faith walk exemplified by Moses, Ruth, Esther, Paul, and many more who went before us into the unknown and provide an example for us of endurance, commitment, love of the Lord, patience, and faith.

Let's dive a little deeper into what it means to walk by faith.

Faith is described as "the confident assurance that what we hope for is going to happen. It is the evidence of things we cannot see."

Many times, we as Christians become frustrated, defeated, or discouraged when we don't feel our needs, desires, and expectations have been met. It's easy to become impatient and quit. Above all, we need to keep our vision on heaven and not get stuck in making accusations of God-Allow Him to love you the way He wants to. I promise you'll find what He has for you is so much more; even if we feel defeated in the present moment because of what we thought our business or life would like at this point.

I want you to take courage from these heroes of faith. "Do not throw away this confident trust in the Lord, no matter what happens. Remember the great reward awaits you.

"Above all, keep your vision on heaven!"

Read

Hebrews 11 | Hebrews 10:35-36
Hebrews 12:1-2 | Galatians 1:10 | Galatians 3

Reflect

What is or has caused you to lose faith? Are there
areas you are doubting or wavering right now?

_____

_____

_____

_____

_____

_____

_____

_____

What can you do to strengthen
your faith muscle?

_____

_____

_____

_____

_____

_____

_____

_____

_____

_____

PRAY

Praise | Repent | Ask | Yay

Father, I thank you for being the same yesterday, today, and tomorrow. I praise you for your unfailing love. Thank you for the lessons I can learn from those who have come before me. Father, forgive me when I am impatient with myself and your timing. Instead of feeling discouraged and frustrated, I want to be filled up with joy, hope, and faith because I know you are working all things out for my good. Through my spirit, I will steward the relationships and opportunities that you place in my path. Thank you Lord for continuing to lead me.

Amen

Are You Wavering?

Day 26

*"Let us hold unswervingly to the hope we pro-
fess, for he who promised is faithful."
Hebrews 10:23*

Making decisions can be so hard. If you're anything like I used to be, you have a tendency to people please, and you don't want to make the wrong decision. You also probably have felt this in your relationship with God. Fear of making the wrong decision and displeasing Him.

However, the Lord has been teaching me that I don't have to try or to earn His love and approval. We were given that with the gift of Jesus when He was sacrificed on the cross for you and for me. Galatians reminds us of this truth. "All who put their faith in Christ share the same blessing Abraham received because of his faith." The old law is gone, and we now have the power of the

Holy Spirit living inside us as our guide. It's time we activate that power and quit wavering in our faith and decisions. The wavering holds you back from stepping into that next version of you.

Therefore, it's important to remember you are already "one with Christ. You are his heir, and now all the promises God gave to Him belong to you."

"It's time we activate the Holy Spirit power living inside us & quit wavering!"

Now you can live in freedom knowing you have already found supernatural favor in the sight of the Lord.

There was a time I was battling my mind and my spirit about a business decision. I was trying to make decisions both from logic and from what the Lord was telling me. My mind kept making me afraid and worried, both things which are not from the Lord. It caused me anxiety and many nights of losing sleep. When we feel this way, we are operating from the Tree of the knowledge of good and evil. Once we become aware of this, we must shift into the Spirit so we can operate from the Tree of Life.

James 1-woke me up to what I needed to do. Quit Wavering! Quit worrying about what everyone else thinks or wants you to do. Don't let fear of failure hold you back. What do you want? What does your spirit say?

David gives us the steps to follow when making decisions as a leader (1 Samuel 23):

> 1. Seek and Ask the Lord
> 2. Listen and do as the Lord tells you *without* doubting
> 3. Ask the Lord and PRAY (vs.10)

The Lord will help you make decisions through asking and praying to him, seeking wise counsel, through Scripture, and through the leading of His Spirit on your heart. Look for where your soul and Spirit find peace.

So if you have been stuck in the wavering, get out of your mind and into your Spirit.

Then ACT with an expectant heart!

"If you're stuck in the wavering, get out of your mind and into your spirit!"

See the miracles the Lord brings your way once you decide without the wavering.

When I acted and made a decision in faith to step into a new level with a new opportunity, I immediately reaped the reward through divine connections and profit.

So move forward in making a decision. You won't get anywhere by staying where you are or teetering back and forth. Operate from the wisdom and abundance that is already yours as a daughter of the King. How good do you believe your Father to be?

Read

Hebrew 10:23 | James 1:5-8 |
1 Samuel 23 | Matthew 9:18-22
Hebrews 12:1-2

Reflect

What decisions have you been afraid to make?

_____

_____

_____

What do you believe God's character to be?

_____

_____

_____

_____

What do you feel your spirit is telling you when you ask the Lord what he wants you to do?

_____

_____

_____

_____

PRAY

Praise | Repent | Ask | Yay

Father, thank you for your Scripture. I praise you for your word that is still alive and relevant to me today to help guide me. I have been wavering, doubting, and afraid of making the wrong decision. I've also been afraid of the unknown or what if I fail. I've been trying to live and work and decide only thinking about my own strength. But Lord, I know that I don't want to do any of this without you. I ask Lord, that you make it clear to my spirit what I should do next. I ask for courage to take steps of faith. I thank you for the blessings and divine connections coming my way. Thank you for trusting me with this kingdom work.

In Your name Jesus, Amen

Are You Searching for A Roadmap?

Day 27

> *"Enter through the narrow gate. For wide is the gate and broad is the road that leads to destruction, and many enter through it."*
> *Matthew 7:13*

I don't know about you, but I've always been someone who likes to have a roadmap and plan of action. I'm willing to do the work, but I like to just be told what to do. Give me the formula, and I will gladly implement it. I think that's why I did so well in school. However, with that thinking, I'm finding that I also make things harder than they need to be. We can't always wait for a clear roadmap or formula. A formula makes life and business too rigid which can bring resistance and perfectionism. This again, is operating from the Tree of the knowledge of good and evil which brings death. We want life! We want to work in flow.

Our relationship with Christ doesn't have to be hard. In fact it's quite simple. Confess with your mouth that He is Lord, repent from your sins, and be in relationship with Him.

Through His death on the cross, when we ask Jesus into our hearts, we are now one with Him. We are given the Holy Spirit. There is nothing we have to do, to strive for, or earn. The gift has been freely given.

But if you're still looking for a roadmap, the Lord provides it:

Trust in the Lord and do good
Take delight in the Lord and Seek Him first
Commit everything you do to the Lord
Be still in the Lord
Do not envy others
Do not worry about tomorrow
Worship & Praise the Lord for what He's done
Wait patiently for the Lord
Pray about everything
Be full of Joy in the Lord

Do these things and you will have peace. "The same God who takes care of me will supply all your needs from his glorious riches, which have been given to us in Christ Jesus." (Philippians 4:19)

As we go through our life and different stages of business, we will have lots of things needing our attention, and we can feel like we are being pulled in all different directions.

That is why it's important to remember your core values and come back to the heart of worship where it's all about Him.

You will be tempted to want to work and do out of your own strength. Resist that urge. Surrender those anxious thoughts, feelings, & worries to the Lord daily. Walk in stride with Him, putting your trust in His will and plan for your life. Simply operate in rest.

Know Him as your God, your Father, your Business Partner, and your Friend. "For where the Spirit of the Lord is, there is freedom."

"When we feel like we're being pulled in all different directions come back to the heart of worhsip where it's all about Him!"

Read

Psalm 37, 40 | Philippians 4
Matthew 6:33 | 2 Corinthians 3:17

1 Thessalonians 1-2

Reflect

Where do you feel rigidity in your life or
business? Where do you feel out of alignment?

_____

_____

_____

_____

_____

_____

_____

Where can you loosen the reins to shift in
oeprating from a place of rest-working in flow
with your spirit?

_____

_____

_____

Spend time in worship and prayer today.
Write down what the Lord speaks to
you during this time.

_____

_____

_____

_____

_____

_____

PRAY

Praise | Repent | Ask | Yay

Amazing and Everlasting Father, how I love you
and adore you. I praise you for your delight in
me. I praise you for your guiding principles that
you show me how to live and to love. Forgive me
when I think too much about the future or what
might be that I fill my thoughts with unnecessary
fears and worries. Help me to be present in your
presence daily. Fill my thoughts with your will
and desires. Thank you for your gospel roadmap
and the gift of your Son, Jesus.

Amen

Purpose In the Pruning

Day 28

"He cuts off every branch in me that bears no fruit, while every branch that does bear fruit he prunes so that it will be even more fruitful."
John 15:2

As you step into your purpose and pursue your calling, you're probably going to experience a lot more ups and downs than you realized. You will be challenged to think that the difficulties you experience might mean you aren't following God's will.

Your first thought will be to think maybe you should quit or say that the enemy is attacking you. Yes, spiritual attacks can & will happen, but I want to challenge that kind of thinking. Let's quit giving the devil so much credit. We can almost use him as a reason not to do the hard work or heart work. Why is it when things get tough, we immediately think it's satan? What if instead, this is part of the pruning process you must go through so you can be prepared to lead and impact more lives? If we keep giving the enemy credit, we might miss the opportunities to bear fruit. It will be easy to want to give up or slow down. Be about the Father's business and respond with the authority you have as an heir of Christ. What would Jesus do? He would activate the Word.

"The pruning process is preparing you to lead and impact more lives."

When challenges come your way, thank the Lord and ask Him, What does this mean? What do you want me to do with this, Lord?

As Steven Furtick teaches, "Our resource is greater than resistance." The only way to fail is to quit. So when the road causes feelings of doubt, resistance, or weariness, we can be like Paul. He rejoiced and found peace in the prison. So you too can find peace and praise in the pruning. What the enemy intends for harm, God intends it for good.

Read

John 15:2 | Acts 16:16-34 | Genesis 50:19-21
Genesis 41:51-52 | John 15:1-5
Philippians 1:6,12-14 | Matthew 4:1-11
Ephesians 6:10-18

Reflect

What 3 areas was Jesus tempted? How did he respond?

_____

_____

_____

_____

_____

_____

_____

_____

_____

What steps do you need to take to clear the space of the old to make room for the new?

_____

PRAY

Praise | Repent | Ask | Yay

Father, thank you for this season of pruning.
I know you are taking me through it to remove
that which is no longer serving me and to create
space for new life. Forgive me for fighting you
at times through this process. It is painful and
uncomfortable and part of me does not want to
trust you and let go. I ask that you give me your
strength, your wisdom, and your peace to take
the steps I need to move forward and step into
the beautiful life you have in store for me. Your
glory and honor will shine through me when you
are done. I surrender all to you.

In your name I pray, Amen.

Becoming a
World Changer

Day 29

"Therefore go and make disciples of all nations, baptizing them in the name of the Father and of the son and of the Holy Spirit, and teaching them to obey everything I have commanded you. And surely I am with you always, to the very end of the age."
Matthew 28: 19-20

B usiness is your passion, but the gospel is your mission. You are called as a Christian to spread the Lord's message of love, peace, rest, surrender, and hope. It just so happens, your mission field is the marketplace. As an entrepreneur, you have a unique opportunity through the marketplace to be a world changer. Just as Esther was created to stand up for her people, you too are made for such a time as this to impact your tribe through your business by being a beacon of light in this seemingly dark world.

How do you do this? How do you shine His light and use your business to share the message of Jesus? Hopefully, you have been taking notes throughout this devotional and have come to realize you have all the pieces you need within you already.

In the beginning of this devotional, you were shown how to find and align your identity as a daughter of the King. By now, you have claimed your crown and are standing in that Holy Spirit empowerment you have been given. With this empowerment, you can go

> *"With Holy Spirit empowerment, you can go confidently into the business world sharing the love of Jesus!"*

confidently into the business world sharing the love of Jesus with those coming into your sphere of influence because through you, they can see Him. This happens through your interactions in messenger, coaching calls, video content, posts, your profile, team cutlure, and your values of integrity, honesty, conistency, and commitment. When you co-labor with Christ and operate in the Spirit, you become magnetic. People will see something different about you and want to be a part of that. That's why you want to align your core values with your business. This in itself will help you stand out because you will be operating from a place of rest, flow, abundance, confidence, and service instead of strife, frustration, resistance, procrastination, perfectionism, and weariness.

You will have a mission driven business that will create Kingdom impact.

Now, you can rise as a leader and step into your ultimate purpose of becoming a world changer. Let's be about that Kingdom hustle. Even if your "world" is a small store front, a social media platform, or a home based business, you have influence. You have everything you need to go out and make disciples.

It's time to Rise to Your Purpose.

"You have everything you need to go out and make disciples."

Read

Matthew 5: 13-16 | Matthew 28: 19-20

Esther 4:14

Reflect

How can you use your business to
share the love of Jesus? What are some tangible

ways to be salt and light?

_____

_____

_____

_____

_____

_____

_____

_____

_____

Where do you need to pivot or make some
tweaks to align to your core values and

create a mission-driven business?

_____

_____

PRAY

Praise | Repent | Ask | Yay

Father, thank you for creating me for such a time as this. I know you are working all things for my good. Let me pursue more of you. I ask that you bring blessings and favor upon my family, myself, and my business. Thank you for your protection and provision as I step up to become a world changer. When people see me, I want them to see you. You are a good, good father. It's in your name I pray, Amen.

Rise to Your Purpose!

Day 30

"Rise up; this matter is in your hands. We will support you, so take courage and do it."
Ezra 10:4

Walk forward as the Fearless Faith Influencer and World Changer God is calling you to be.

It's time to rise sister! You know your mission field, your mission, and your purpose as a daughter of the one true King. Rise and stand firm in this empowerment. When we rise to our purpose, we rise together as one body of believers, and that's how Kingdom impact is created. Together, we are bolder, braver, and stronger.

You have talents, gifts, and strengths that the world needs to experience. You have a fire and a message in your heart that the world needs to hear. We need you, dear sister, to rise up, claim your crown, align your business to God's path for you, and take imperfect action. You don't have to have it all figured out right now. Just be your authentic self and take at least one action step daily.

You are worthy of love. You are worthy of success. You are worthy of abundance. You have the victory as "more than conquerers through Christ." He has made you the CEO of His business. So "be fruitful and multiply." One of the most important parts of being a Christian will be the kind of influence you have on others. As Wayne Cordeiro writes, "The goal is to get the salt out of the saltshaker and into the world. He

"When we rise to our purpose, we rise together as one, and that's how kingdom impact is created!"

will hold us accountable for how much we have done of what He has asked us to do. We cannot forget our assignment." (Author of *Jesus, Pure and Simple*)

Read

Ezra 10:4 | 2 Peter 1:10-11 | Romans 8:29
Ephesians 4:1-6, 11-16 | 1 Peter 5:1-11

Genesis 1:28

Reflect

What imperfect action can you take next
to rise to your purpose?

_____

_____

_____

_____

_____

_____

_____

_____

_____

_____

Who is in your circle you can rise with?

_____

_____

_____

_____

_____

_____

PRAY

Praise | Repent | Ask | Yay

Father, thank you for equipping me with everything I need to take action and rise to the purpose you have called me to. Forgive me for playing small at times and giving into the lies of the enemy who only wants to kill, steal, and destroy the beautiful life you want to give me.

I ask for strength as I step out in imperfect action and walk the path that you are guiding me to walk. Over and over again, you show me that I am loved and supported by you if only I come to you for guidance. I surrender this life, this business, and this journey to you and your ways. Together, we will create a mission driven business with kingdom impact and rise to claim your victory. In your name, Jesus, I pray this prayer confidently.

Amen.

Closing Letter from Brandie and Natalie

(Listen to the song, "The Blessing")

Dear Sister,

Thank you for reading this devotional and spending the last thirty days with us. We pray blessing and favor over you, your family, and your business.

We pray that these last thirty days have brought you closer in your relationship with God, that you have stepped into your identity, and that you are thriving in your life and business. It is our hope that you have aligned your business with your core values to set yourself up for a life of flow, abundance, and service instead of burnout and worldly strife.

You have been chosen, and we pray you use your passion for business and your mission for the gospel to rise up as a leader and shine your light in the business world! Let's walk in the victory of Christ.

We leave you with this blessing prayed over you:

The Lord bless you
And keep you
May His face shine upon you
And be gracious to you
The Lord turn His
Face toward you
And give you peace

May His favor be upon you
And a thousand generations
Your family and your children
And their children, and their children

Now rise up!

xoxo

Your fellow sisters and purpose partners,

Brandie & Natalie

P.S. We want you to dream God sized dreams. You never know what the Lord will do through you.

"Sarah wanted a baby. God wanted her to birth a nation. Stop thinking small.

Brandie and Natalie are both married & live in Indiana. They have always been women of faith pursuing their God sized dreams. After starting their careers in Business Admin and Education, Brandie & Natalie partnered with a new company in the network-marketing industry. They quickly ranked to the top 2% of their company, but hit the "wall" of burnout as they faded into the "copy/paste" world.

About Brandie & Natalie

Their inner mean girls turned on them. They began doubting their worth and losing their passion. Once they aligned their business with their faith, that's when everything changed. The Lord gave them the vision for Victorious Entreperneurs Rising where women of faith in the marketplace could find their voice and rise as leaders.

Rise to Your Purpose signature course and podcast were formed to partner, mentor, and collaborate with other Kingdom driven women in the industry. Therefore, alongside their Network Marketing businesses, they also coach women on how to build profitable mission driven businesses from a place of rest. They would love to have you connect with them and join their community.

"Choosing to understand &
embrace who you are is one of the
most unselfish things you can do be-
cause it maximizes your ability toserve
others & bring glory to God."
~ Holley Gerth

Bonuses

**We hope to continue partnering with
you in faith and business!**

FREE resources:

1. Creating Your Scripture-Based
Daily Affirmations

2. Building Your Kingdom Impact Network
Marketing Business

3. Rise to Your Purpose Spotify Playlist

*www.VictoriousEntrepreneursRising/***Bonus**

CPSIA information can be obtained
at www.ICGtesting.com
Printed in the USA
BVHW042133281121
622752BV00012B/468